G000065555

Medieval Dartmoor

PAUL WHITE

Bossiney Books · Launceston

First published 2001 by Bossiney Books
Langore, Launceston, Cornwall PL15 8LD
ISBN 1-899383-43-3
The photograph on page 21 is by Roy Westlake.
All other photographs are by the author. The artwork is by Graham Hallowell.
Printed in Great Britain by R Booth (Troutbeck Press), Mabe, Cornwall

Medieval Dartmoor

This book suggests a number of places on Dartmoor which you will hopefully find worth a visit, covering various aspects of medieval life such as farming and industry, housing and religion. Ordnance Survey grid references are given: the 1:25,000 Outdoor Leisure Map is definitely worth buying.

When were 'the Middle Ages'? Historical periods are of course just a retrospective invention of historians. Academics have fun debating when periods began or ended, in terms of social or cultural change. Political or dynastic changes – such as the battles in 1066 and 1485 which (for the English alone!) used to define the Middle Ages – are now thought less significant. The Saxons and Danes are part of 'early medieval'. For Dartmoor, the Dissolution of the monasteries in 1539 created an entirely new economic climate. So this book will rather arbitrarily – and very superficially! – cover the period AD550-1550.

Dartmoor has been exploited by people for some 6000 years. For much of that time the higher ground was probably used mostly for summer grazing, but there have been a few periods when areas of it were settled and cultivated – notably the Bronze Age and the Middle Ages, especially from about AD900-1350. Climate change and population pressures were the decisive factors.

Dartmoor's upland population was already far smaller in Roman times than it had been 1500 years earlier. Then in the sixth century a series of plagues swept through Europe, and seem to have afflicted south-western Britain and Wales particularly badly.

One intriguing possibility is that dust clouds from a massive eruption of Krakatoa around AD540 created a 'volcanic winter', bringing famine, weakness and disease as an inevitable consequence. But what is fairly certain is that at about this time substantial numbers emigrated from Devon and Cornwall to Brittany, which was underpopulated and had suffered less from the plague.

Opposite: the medieval hamlet of Hound Tor

Challacombe, not far from Grimspound. In certain lights, especially in winter, the remains of a medieval field system can be clearly seen. A small settlement now stands where once there was a village

It seems likely that the whole of Devon was very thinly populated for several centuries afterwards. Into this near-deserted landscape came 'Saxon' settlers from Wessex, who easily found good quality land which had been abandoned. It is possible that the settlement of Devon was mainly peaceful, although there were battles later on either side of the river Tamar. There was no immediate need to re-colonise Dartmoor.

We have insufficient evidence either archaeological or historical to know exactly how and when the Saxons settled around or on the Moor. The old idea that fair-haired German warriors with their families and descendants invaded Britain and forced 'the Celts' into the western and northern hills is now doubted by most historians. There may even have been as few as 50,000 'Saxon' immigrants in the whole of England, but they were disproportionately powerful.

Early Wessex probably contained very few of these immigrants. Its people had once spoken 'British' (which became Welsh/Cornish/ Breton) and a bit of Latin if they were gentry or merchants. Now they adopted the new economically dominant language – 'Anglo-Saxon'. Dumnonia (the British kingdom of Devon and Cornwall) lost control of Devon to Wessex somewhere between AD 650 and 700.

At this time it is likely that the whole Dartmoor area was almost uninhabited, with just a few farming families (probably British-speaking) eking out a living on its borders. The only substantial settlement known was at Lydford, where the church is dedicated to St Petrock, a 'Celtic' saint, which suggests an origin before 650. By 900 it had become a Saxon *burh* (defended town), one of only four in Devon, and in 977 it withstood a Viking raiding force which sacked Tavistock Abbey.

By the time of Domesday Book in 1086, although the centre of the moor (the royal 'Forest') was still uninhabited, farms such as Natsworthy (SX 721800) were being ploughed at 370 metres altitude. The Saxon period saw a great extension of agriculture into areas which had been abandoned for the previous 1500 years, and this continued after 1066. The expansion was propelled by population growth and assisted by an improving climate.

But by 1300 the climate was again worsening. Medieval farmers had to be self-sufficient. As well as tending animals, they had to grow corn and vegetables. This became harder as rainfall levels increased. When the Black Death struck in 1348-9 and a third of the population died, land at lower altitudes became available which could be cultivated with less risk of crop failures. The oppressive system which tied workers to the land began to crumble, allowing many to escape.

Many hamlets and farmsteads – if they had not already been abandoned – were deserted at this time or within the next fifty years. Yet many medieval settlements were not abandoned: some were deserted in later centuries, but many still exist today. Occasionally the original buildings survive, perhaps as farm outbuildings.

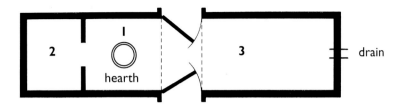

1: Living room or 'livier' **2:** working area **3:** shippon

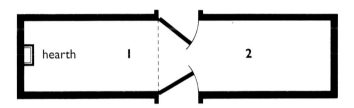

Simplified ground-plans of longhouse (top) and of cross-passage house (below)

Longhouses

The characteristic medieval Dartmoor building is the longhouse. The earliest surviving examples can be seen at two excavated and beautifully presented medieval hamlets, Hound Tor (SX746788) and Hutholes (SX702759). At these abandoned sites it is possible to get some idea of how life must have been around 1300.

Longhouses were built on a slope, and combined living quarters for people (locally known as the 'livier') at the upper end, and for animals (the 'shippon') at the lower end, with a sluice drain in the lower end wall. The longhouse was single storey. Its livier was often just one room, as was the shippon, and the division between them was not necessarily a wall of full height. It is reckoned that a cow puts out as much heat as a single-bar electric fire and this heat was very welcome. Given no windows and a peat fire smoking on the central hearth, it must have been truly cosy!

The Hutholes settlement contains several longhouses. That shown above was a very substantial building. In the one shown below, the cooking hearth can be seen at the far end on the left

The entrance or entrances served man and beast alike. In later examples, an inner room is found – not, as you might imagine, a bedroom, but of more practical use as a storeroom or dairy – and 'outshot' or lean-to rooms might be added still later.

The other common type of medieval farmhouse is the 'cross passage house' in which there is a living room at either end, and a cross passage between a front door and a back door – with the animals in a separate building outside. It was possible for a house to be converted from one style to the other. Animals might be expelled to a separate building as a family grew richer.

At Hound Tor the largest longhouse, often referred to as the 'manor house', is the one furthest from the Hound Tor rocks, 17.5 metres long by just 4 metres wide and divided into three rooms. The livier has an inner room and the shippon has a central drain. But this building was originally constructed as a two room cross-passage house, and was subsequently converted to accommodate the cattle in the former living room. Perhaps the family fortunes had declined. Or had the 'squire' moved downhill to a more sheltered location, leaving his old house to junior members of the family?

The four Hound Tor longhouses and their outbuildings were built in the 13th century, and replaced earlier buildings, probably of turf which was used when wood was unavailable. The manor was owned by Tavistock Abbey and included at least one other small settlement with a longhouse and barns (SX 745791).

Domesday Book tells us that in 1086 Hound Tor's tenant under the Abbot was Rainald (who also held many other manors): at Hound Tor he had two slaves and two 'villeins' (villagers) working for him, and there were also four 'bordars' (smallholders). Women and children were not enumerated. None of them were free to leave this land. There were also 2 ploughs, 7 cattle, 28 sheep and 12 goats.

Longhouses are not unique to Dartmoor, but here they survive in larger numbers than elsewhere – more than a hundred are known. This is probably because they were built of enduring granite at a

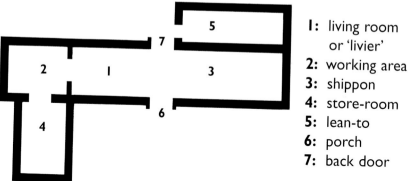

1: living room or 'livier'
2: working area
3: shippon
4: store-room
5: lean-to
6: porch
7: back door

One of the longhouses at Hound Tor, with a sketch plan

time of relative prosperity, then survived centuries of poverty and so were neither replaced nor converted beyond recognition. Sometimes the whole of the old longhouse was used for farm purposes while a new range or a cross-wing was added at the upper end.

Early Dartmoor Farmhouses by Elizabeth Gawne and Jenny Sanders can be thoroughly recommended for further reading.

Two surviving longhouses: above, Ollsbrim (SX688734)

Below, Hole Farm (SX685861)

Farming

In the photograph above it is just possible to see the typical vestiges of medieval ploughing at Hound Tor – parallel ridge and furrow marks. These identify strips of land which 'belonged' to different families. The ploughman circled round the strip, and the mould-board of the plough threw the soil up to one side, forming a ridge in the middle and furrows either side. The furrows helped drain the land. It was a survival strategy: in a drought a crop might survive in the damp furrow, in a wet year the plants on the ridge would do best.

The fields would have been worked communally, whatever the exact details of 'ownership' of the crops on each strip. These people must have been totally dependent on each other – and the agreeable lifestyle of Rainald and the abbots of Tavistock depended on them.

Part of their work was to wrest additional arable land from the 'waste', or hitherto unfarmed land. Although they needed to grow their own crops, their main business would have been their sheep, goats and cattle which grazed on the unenclosed moor in summer.

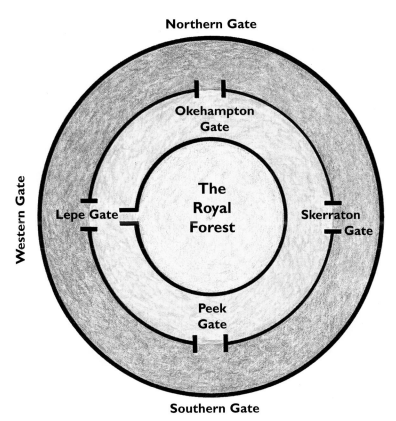

The original of this map states: 'The inner circle represents the Forest and is held in common by all. The second circle represents the moors from the Forest to the enclosures. The outer circle represents the private lands within the enclosures, tilled and inhabited'

Medieval maps of Dartmoor showed the moor schematically as concentric circles: the diagram above is based on a map of about 1550 which has been re-drawn and the text edited for clarity (taking some liberties in the process: the original appears in a fascinating book, *Early Devon Maps* by Mary Ravenhill and Margery Rowe).

Another agricultural activity which has left relics on Dartmoor is the rabbit warren. These were quite numerous, always owned by a nobleman or a religious house, and usually looked after by a warrener one of whose duties must have been to prevent poaching.

The warren consisted of a number of 'pillow mounds' in which earth was piled up in sufficient quantity for a colony of rabbits to feel safe inside. Burrowing in this loose, well drained earth must have been rather easier than on the natural moor. Cleverly designed traps were built to ensnare vermin.

The schematic structure of a parish. The population lives at or near the lowest point. Above the village are its open fields, as well as enclosed land belonging to individuals. Above that is an area of pasture to which only the villagers have grazing rights. Above that again, beyond the parish boundary, is 'The Forest' in which almost everyone in Devon had grazing rights

to Forest

Unenclosed pasture belonging to the parish

Common fields and private land of the parish

*Left: this track leads steeply down to the east of Cosdon Beacon,
running between enclosed fields. Today it serves to take walkers to the
high ground without disturbing the farmers – an ancient function,
regardless of the age of this particular path*

Right: the old track on Yartor Down

Communications

At a very early period – probably in the Bronze Age – drove roads
were established which allowed outsiders access to the high moor
without disturbing the village communities on its fringes. Every
farmer in Devon seems to have had grazing rights on Dartmoor –
except the burghers of Barnstaple and Totnes. Yet more tracks led
from the village onto its own part of the moor.

Many of these tracks still survive in one form or another. One of
the most evocative I have walked is that which leads from near South

Brent (you can pick it up at SX 684603) to Corringdon Ball Gate.

Medieval Dartmoor was no 'trackless waste'. It was criss-crossed with paths and tracks suitable for people on foot or horseback, for trains of pack animals, or for loads pulled on sledges. Wheeled vehicles were not used in most parishes until the nineteenth century.

Some of the long-distance tracks can still be traced today: the photograph opposite shows part of a track on Yartor Down, above Dartmeet (park at SX 680733 and walk due east) showing the typical hollow created by centuries of use.

Half way up the hill from Dartmeet (SX 677733) stands the Coffin Stone. When someone died in this part of the Forest, their corpse had to be carried to Widecombe Church along the Lich Path. (Before 1260 it had to be carried all the way to Lydford, which in winter was 25 km or 15 miles further than Widecombe!)

It was traditional even into the twentieth century to rest the coffin on the Coffin Stone. Legend tells that the stone was cloven in two by a lightning bolt when a particularly sinful corpse was resting there: one hopes the bearers were not too close at hand!

The Coffin Stone, on the hill east of Dartmeet

The two bridges at Postbridge, a medieval clapper bridge, and behind it the turnpike trust's bridge of the 1770s, on the newly constructed post-road from Exeter to Tavistock and on to Truro and Falmouth

Our ancestors generally chose the straight route to walk up or down a hill: the zig-zag approach, reducing the gradient, only came in when roads were reconstructed for wheeled traffic, often in the eighteenth or early nineteenth century, and at many places in Devon you can spot the old track plunging headlong downhill as a bridle-way while the tarmac road snakes back and forth across the hillside.

The river crossing might be a ford or a clapper bridge, a primitive structure heavy enough to resist the river when it is in violent flood. Most of the clapper bridges seen today are unlikely to be original, but are probably replacements for earlier and similar structures. Even modern bridges can be destroyed by floods, so it is amazing any clapper bridges have survived at all.

Everything must have been new some time. 'New Bridge', like nearby Holne Bridge, was 'new' around 1415. Building bridges of

New Bridge, once known as 'New Holne Bridge' (SX 711709)

this quality was clearly a major expense and presumably done at a time of great prosperity in the tin and/or cloth industries.

Medieval bridges were often constructed by wealthy people at the suggestion of priests or monks: it was very good for the soul – an assured quick route to heaven. No better way of funding roads and bridges was found until the mid-eighteenth century, when turnpikes promised investors a direct route to more earthly profits.

This longhouse lies on an ancient route which used to go straight through the building, between the livier and the shippon! The house was probably once a hostelry for travellers

Above: Siward's Cross, also known as Nun's Cross, presumably named after Siward, Earl of Northumberland, who owned a manor in Mary Tavy just before the Norman Conquest

Below: Brentor Church, said to have been built in fulfilment of a vow in the 13th century – and a landmark across much of West Devon

Left: Ollsbroom Cross (SX685735), a crossroad marker restored to its proper place. It lost its arms while serving as a farm gatepost
Right: the magnificent early Christian cross on Sourton village green

Another helpful but rather cheaper way to save your soul was by erecting a cross as a waymark, and these are numerous on Dartmoor. They were doubly useful if placed where two tracks crossed, or if they marked a parish or estate boundary as well as the line of a track. Some may have had a previous existence as ancient standing stones and been reshaped to proclaim the new faith.

Other crosses around the moor served a different purpose. They were set up in settlements before a church had been built, perhaps in the sacred enclosure (*lan* in the British language): the churchyard as an enclosure often pre-dates the church. Other crosses were established as village preaching points, and after the church had been built they sometimes became the secular centre of the village.

A surviving gateway of Tavistock Abbey, 'Betsy Grimbal's Tower'. The Abbey covered a large part of what is now central Tavistock: indeed the town grew up to serve the abbey and was dominated by it until the Dissolution of the monasteries in 1539 – after which the Russell family, Dukes of Bedford, acquired the Abbey's estates. They in turn benevolently dominated the town until the early twentieth century

Abbeys and churches

The Church played an important part in medieval life on the secular level as well as the religious. The three abbeys of Tavistock, Buckfast and Buckland, the very wealthy priory at Plympton and the Bishop of Exeter owned vast amounts of land, including many of the villages on the borders of Dartmoor. Tavistock Abbey's annual income was little short of £1000 at the Dissolution of the monasteries: this compares with the Devon income of the richest south-west landowner at the time, Henry Courtenay, which was £1300.

Tavistock Abbey was founded in the 970s. Its buildings covered a huge area – most of what is today central Tavistock. Only fragments remain, including the gateway now known as 'Betsy Grimbal's Tower' and the wall and Still Tower beside the river. There had been a small settlement at Tavistock before the monks arrived, but it was the abbot who initiated the Friday market and annual fair and around 1160 had it made into a borough.

Buckland Abbey lies just off the moor today, near Yelverton, but the unenclosed moor extended much further when it was founded, in 1278. After the Dissolution some of the abbey buildings, including a wonderful barn, survived as part of Sir Richard Grenville's country house, which was bought by Sir Francis Drake in 1581. It is now a National Trust property.

Buckland Abbey, a Cistercian house, came into the possession of Sir Richard Grenville and was later bought by Sir Francis Drake, newly wealthy and newly knighted after his circumnavigation voyage

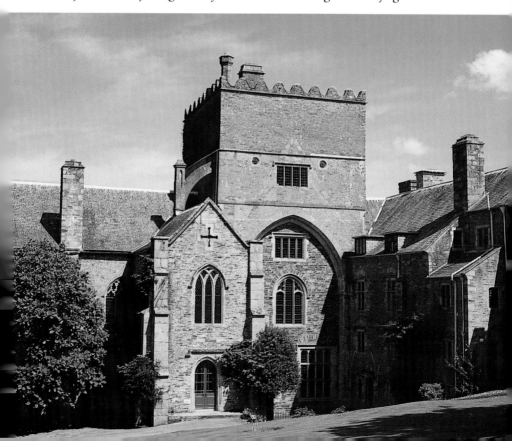

Buckfast Abbey was founded in 1018 by King Cnut. By 1100 it had ceased to exist but was refounded 1134-6 as a Cistercian house. Its annual income at the Dissolution was £486. Buckfast was refounded as a modern Benedictine Abbey in 1902, and a new church was built. The rejuvenated Abbey attracts many visitors.

All the medieval abbeys exploited their vast properties much as contemporary secular owners did – but often with greater skill. They farmed manors, founded borough towns and encouraged the growth of local industries, all with a view to maximising their incomes.

The abbeys in Devon, as elsewhere, were mainly founded by kings. Early abbots were often a member of the royal family who had been 'offered' to the Church as a child. His family expected him to live in style becoming to his birth and the abbey had to be endowed with great estates to make this possible. It is quite likely that the re-colonisation of Dartmoor in the tenth century stemmed at least in part from grants of under-used royal land to the abbeys, and the abbots' wish to make the most of their new property.

The spiritual needs of the population outside the monastic walls were the responsibility not of the abbeys, but of the bishop and the parish clergy.

There is much medieval work to be seen in the churches – enough to require a separate book. The photograph on the right shows the church and church house at Widecombe-in-the-Moor, a huge parish. From 1260 this church also served the inhabitants of the eastern side of the Forest, who should theoretically have gone to Lydford church – all 22,700 hectares (56,000 acres) of the Forest were part of Lydford parish until 1987.

Because long walks to church were quite normal, church houses were built to accommodate the parishioners between services, and to provide refreshments. Naturally they became a focus of village life and in many Devon villages they have been preserved as the village inn. That at Widecombe was built in 1537, and now houses a National Trust shop and a room which serves as a village hall.

These scars in the hillside near Challacombe (and directly opposite Grimspound) are the remains of tin-working, where the tinners cut back into the hillside in a methodical manner to locate and extract tin ore. This method began in the late medieval period, but these particular workings – in their present form – are post-medieval

The tin industry

Tin was discovered on Dartmoor about AD 1150; for the next fifty years it was a very important industry, and was worked under special Stannary Laws (Latin *stannum* = tin) which both taxed the trade and at the same time gave the tinners privileges and encouragement.

The subject is a complicated one, and the following account is highly simplified. Readers wanting to explore it further might start with Phil Newman's *The Dartmoor Tin Industry, A field guide* (1998).

In the early days the only method of obtaining the ore was by 'streaming'. By scouring the stream beds, the tinners found black stones containing tin ore, or they could pan gravel for it, rather like prospectors in the Gold Rush. The tin ore (cassiterite) is far heavier than other rock, so it can be separated by gravity if the gravel is swirled around in water.

The ore was then crushed using horizontal round millstones in a building called a crazing-house: the technique was borrowed from corn-milling. The ore was crudely smelted on site, then transported to a 'stannary town' for further smelting under official supervision. Chagford, Ashburton, Plympton and Tavistock were the stannary towns, each with jurisdiction over a sector of the moor.

For a few years in the 1180s Devon was a major player in the world tin market, but the virgin deposits were soon used up. Production fell steeply so new methods were gradually introduced to improve the yields. The tinners sought out the 'lodes' from which the ore in the stream-beds had been broken, and followed them back into the hillside, creating great scars down the hill like those in the photograph (which at least in their present form are post-medieval). They dug test pits in likely areas, many of which proved barren and were left unfilled. Much of today's apparently natural Dartmoor landscape is in reality the half-healed scars of the tin industry.

Once the ore began to be brought out as rock rather than gravel, machinery was invented to break it up. On page 26 you can see the method in use from about 1300-1580, the 'dry stamps'. An overshot waterwheel powers a row of metal-shod poles which rise and fall onto a stone base, crushing the ore. Smelting was now turned into a single process, carried out on the moor in a 'blowing house'. The 'blowing' refers to bellows, powered by a water wheel, which raised the temperature in a furnace fuelled by charcoal, made from peat.

Some of the best examples of blowing houses are those at Merrivale. The first 'Lower Merrivale blowing house' is at SX 553755 and its ruins are shown in the photograph opposite.

Tin ore was delivered to the uphill end of the building (on the right of the photo). The two upright slabs set in the cross-wall are the remains of the furnace. Tipped up at an angle is a 'floatstone' (apparently one of only two to survive) which should be flat, and in which there is a shallow trough. The molten ore dribbled out into

Dry stamps in operation, driven by a water wheel

The Lower Merrivale blowing mill

that trough and was then ladled into the 'mould stone' (today full of rain-water). The ingot of tin was then allowed to cool in the mould, ready to be transported to a stannary town for taxation.

At the next blowing house, SX 553762, you will find much the same arrangement but with a clearly defined water-wheel pit. There is a further pair of buildings – a 'knocking mill' with stamps and a blowing house – at SX 552766 if you are feeling energetic.

All three Merrivale sites were probably active in the period 1500-1550, when there was a minor boom in Dartmoor tin production, though they may have continued into the 17th century. Very sensibly production ceased in the winter months!

The importance of water in powering this industry can hardly be exaggerated. Each waterwheel required a leat (artificial watercourse) to deliver a constant flow of water. Everywhere you walk on Dartmoor you will find leats, some ancient and dry, some still flowing, winding along the contours to a mystery destination.

The tinners were so favoured by successive monarchs that they were no longer answerable, in most things, to the same law-code as other people. They had their own Parliament, their own laws and their own courts. Woe betide a non-tinner who got caught up in the 'justice' of the stannary courts at Lydford.

The tinners' independence was such that when Richard Strode, Plympton's MP in the 1512 Westminster Parliament, tried to stop mining near the seaports because the waste created was choking the harbours, he found himself locked up in the notorious stannary prison of Lydford Castle (which you can still visit – no fee).

There was an ancient rhyme which ran:

> I have heard of Lydford law
> Where in the morn they hang and draw
> And sit in judgement after.

It probably referred to much earlier courts which applied the harsh Forest Law, but the stannary courts did their best to follow the same principles! Don't miss Lydford church or the wonderful Gorge.

Lydford Castle, once the administrative centre for Dartmoor

Now for one of the most bizarre features of medieval Dartmoor – Crockern Tor (SX 616758). This not very distinctive tor is near the road and makes an easy climb with pleasant views, but it was once the venue at which the stannary parliaments met.

The stannary boundaries converged just a little further south but the tor is roughly equidistant from each of the stannary towns. The earliest meeting recorded here was in 1494. Nearly a hundred representatives used to meet on the summit, with the Vice-Warden of the Stannaries in the chair (metaphorically).

It is likely that most men who actually got their hands dirty in the tin industry were part-timers, combining streaming with farm-work. The representatives at the stannary parliaments, on the other hand, were usually landowners and merchants from the towns.

Of the four stannaries, Chagford was the most important until the 1460s, when Ashburton took over until the end of our period. In the post-medieval period, Tavistock grew increasingly important.

South Zeal from Cosdon Hill, showing its fossilised medieval town plan with long thin burgage plots extending back from the main road

The growth of towns

Most towns started as speculative ventures. Land-owners hoped they could make more profit by renting land in towns to 'burghers', with a weekly market and an annual fair, than by renting or farming the land on which the town stood. The embryo town was laid out methodically in 'burgage plots', usually long thin strips running back from a road. The road frontage, where the burgher could set up a shop front, was what made the land valuable.

If the new town was a success, further roads were built and the long plots might be sub-divided, with new roads parallel to the first. Many 'towns' never developed beyond village status and here the initial plan may be visible – as it is in South Zeal which is still part of the parish of South Tawton. It is hard to believe that South Zeal once lay on the main Exeter to Okehampton road.

The 1:25,000 OS map shows clearly its remarkable layout, which is oddly not visible at all on the 1:50,000. If you climb up Cosdon Beacon (and it is quite a climb, to 550 m, 1800 ft) you can see how South Zeal's gardens are still long and thin. On a particularly fine day you can, I believe, see from Cosdon both the English Channel and the Bristol Channel, as well as the beautiful Bronze Age triple stone row at SX 643916 if you still need tempting!

At Tavistock and Ashburton woollen cloth was manufactured from the local Dartmoor wool, and both towns benefited from the twice yearly 'coinages' of tin, as did Chagford. Lydford was more important than it now is, being the administrative centre for the royal Forest. Okehampton was tiny, dependent on its baronial castle. Moreton-hampstead and Bovey Tracey, technically 'boroughs', probably did not develop into real towns until the late 16th century.

Not one of these 'towns' had a total population over 500 and apart from their churches they now have little to see of medieval date but much from later, more dynamic stages of their history. Chagford, though, has a 'medieval feel' and some early Tudor buildings.

To most of those living on medieval Dartmoor, widely spread out over all except the very highest blanket bogs, the surrounding towns would have been all but unknown. For them the communal fields, communal grazing, and a little digging for tin in the hope of striking it rich, would have been the extent of their horizons.

The medieval chapel at South Zeal. The parish church and church house at nearby South Tawton are particularly worth a visit

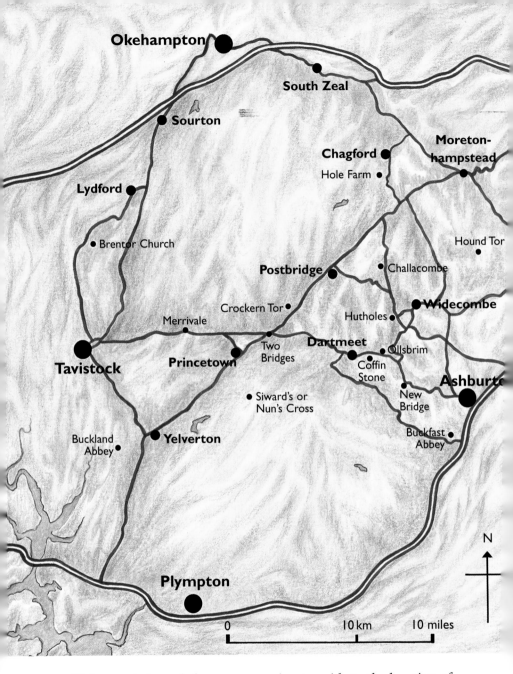

Okehampton

South Zeal

Sourton

Chagford

Moreton-
hampstead

Hole Farm

Lydford

Brentor Church

Hound Tor

Postbridge

Challacombe

Crockern Tor

Widecombe

Merrivale

Hutholes

Two
Bridges

Dartmeet

Ollsbrim

Tavistock

Princetown

Coffin
Stone

Ashburton

Siward's or
Nun's Cross

New
Bridge

Buckland
Abbey

Yelverton

Buckfast
Abbey

N

Plympton

0   10 km   10 miles

This map is intended as an approximate guide to the location of
sites mentioned – not to the relative size of places in the Middle Ages